Original title:
The Lemon's Smile

Copyright © 2025 Creative Arts Management OÜ
All rights reserved.

Author: Lila Davenport
ISBN HARDBACK: 978-1-80586-243-7
ISBN PAPERBACK: 978-1-80586-715-9

Hues of Zest

In the grove where laughter sings,
Yellow orbs with joyful swings,
They dangle low, a cheeky tease,
Beneath the trees, they dance with ease.

A twist of joy in every bite,
Pucker up, what a delight!
Jokes abound, citrusy cheer,
Making each laugh ring clear.

Sunlight's Liquid Bliss

Droplets glisten, playful hue,
Sipping sunshine, the world anew,
A splash of folly in each glass,
Oh, how the sour moments pass!

A wink, a giggle, fizzy thrill,
Every sip, my heart does fill,
With bubbly joy and citrus zest,
In this world, we're truly blessed.

Aromas of Brightness

Fragrant wafts of silly fun,
Frolicking scents, the day's begun,
In every twist, a chuckle hides,
Citrus charm that joy provides.

A burst of laughter, golden rays,
In every flavor, humor plays,
Bitter notes? Oh, not today!
Let's squeeze the gloom and toss away!

Citrus Reverie

In dreams of zest, we find our muse,
Bright and quirky, we choose to cruise,
Twisted tales of the yellow orb,
With giggles that we can absorb.

Rolling laughter, citrus bites,
Each moment's filled with pure delights,
We dance through life, a joyful spree,
In the sun's glow, just you and me.

Nautical Citrus Voyage

On a boat sailing seas so bright,
A fruit with zest takes flight.
It rolls with waves, a merry sight,
Tickling sailors, a burst of light.

The captain laughs, his hat askew,
While crewmates follow, the sea's bright hue.
A playful twist, a fruity brew,
As laughter echoes, the breeze anew.

Sweetness in Every Slice

Slice by slice, the joy begins,
With giggles and grins, the fun never thins.
Each piece a laugh, the juice it spins,
In sunshine's glow, where sweetness wins.

Pies and tarts with zest on top,
Bouncing flavors, can't just stop.
A citrus party, come join the hop,
With every bite, the laughter pops!

Gleeful Yellow Whispers

In gardens bright, whispers of cheer,
Golden orbs shine bright and clear.
They tell the tales that all can hear,
Of sunny days and juice so dear.

With a giggle and a squirt, oh what fun,
Bouncing together, like rays of sun.
A zestful tune, we laugh and run,
In every corner, happiness spun.

Refreshing Breeze of Joy

A cool breeze blows, a citrus fling,
Tickling noses, making hearts sing.
In this fresh air, let laughter cling,
A playful dance with each zingy swing.

On sandy shores, with drinks in hand,
Joyful moments, oh so grand.
A splash, a laugh, on sunny land,
With fruity treats, life's lovely band.

Dappled Sunshine in Green

In the garden, a twisty grin,
Yellow rays dance on a whim.
With laughter and zest in the air,
Things don't seem so dire; they care.

Bees buzzing, wearing tiny hats,
Fruit haters find it a total spats.
Who knew sour could be such fun?
A jester's fruit under the sun.

Trees chuckle with every breeze,
Nature's humor puts us at ease.
Pick a slice, let the jokes unfold,
A tale of zest and joy retold.

Happiness in every drop,
Sweet giggles, never a stop.
Dappled yellow, undergreen,
A sight of laughter, so serene.

Luminous Flavors

Between the dishes and the cheer,
A splash of yellow, never fear.
Tasty giggles on every plate,
A shining fruit that captivates.

Sippers slurping, eyes so wide,
Juicy drips, let's take a ride!
Flavors brightening the gray day,
With laughter to keep the gloom at bay.

In punch bowls, the tang does dance,
A citrus tang ignites romance.
Unexpected zest in every sip,
With a winking smile on each lip.

From the market, a joyful spree,
Bouncing fruit, so wild and free.
In every twist, a laughter burst,
With luminous flavors, quench the thirst!

A Melody of Citrus Bliss

In a bowl, a bright brigade,
Orange laughter, sunshine made.
Twirling slices sing a song,
Peel the past, let joy be strong.

Dancing on the kitchen counter,
Zest-filled moments, never flatter.
Rolling giggles flap their wings,
While the wily fruit simply sings.

Pies and cakes parade in light,
Every bite, a sheer delight.
Citrus notes in harmony,
With a twist, absurdity!

Gather round, let's taste the fun,
Happiness bursting with each pun.
With a smile that brightens the day,
In citrus dreams, let's laugh and sway.

Dewy Smiles at Dawn

Morning dew on citrus bright,
Wakes the fruits with pure delight.
Sunrise paints a cheeky grin,
Nature giggles, let the fun begin!

Chubby cheeks of yellow hue,
Dance with light, a jolly crew.
With every splash, the laughter flows,
Tickling tails on trees it shows.

Froggy hops and buzzing bees,
Join the zest in playful breeze.
Bouncing rays make shadows play,
Harvest joys in a silly way.

Jesters dressed in vibrant skin,
Swing and sway, delight within.
Dewy smiles as day breaks clear,
In this garden, joy is near!

Sweet Peels

Peels that twist in silly curls,
Wrap the laughs of little whirls.
Bouncing laughter, tangy cheer,
Sweet surprise floods atmosphere.

Packing sunshine in each slice,
Zesty quirks that taste so nice.
Slipping on the laughter's zest,
In this fruit bowl, we are blessed.

Squeeze a giggle, drop a smile,
Tangy jokes that stretch for miles.
Reaching up for every cheer,
Sweetness wrapped, it's crystal clear!

Yellow peels, a game of glows,
Silly faces, laughter flows.
In this slice of sunny fun,
Joyful moments, never done!

Chasing Citrus Daydreams

In a dream where fruits take flight,
Citrus creatures dance in light.
Zooming through a sky of cheer,
Silly giggles echo near.

Chasing tails of zestful hues,
With each bounce, the laughter brews.
Springing forth in bursts of fun,
Daydreams shine like morning sun.

Frolicking on the playful breeze,
Bouncing 'round like clumsy bees.
Every wedge a wink and sway,
In this world, we laugh and play.

Dreamy skies of citrus smells,
Telling tales as laughter swells.
Chasing dreams where joy increases,
In the dance, our spirit ceases!

Garden of Grins

In a garden where fruits collide,
Cheeky seeds push dreams aside.
Silly roots that stretch and grin,
Bringing joy from deep within.

Bubblegum skies with pelting rays,
Ticklish leaves that sway and play.
With a bounce, they share delight,
Laughter blooms in soft sunlight.

Peeking through the patchy greens,
Giggles rise like swishing streams.
Splashes of color with every shake,
In the garden, no mistake!

Whirling in this playful scene,
Every fruit brings forth a sheen.
Garden grins as far as the eye,
In laughter's bloom, we watch it fly!

Tints of Happiness

In a bright kitchen, a fruit takes stage,
With a grinning face, it's all the rage.
A splash of yellow, a burst of light,
It tickles our tongues, a pure delight.

Rolling around, oh what a show,
Wobbling and giggling, it's on the go.
Juicy jokes spill with every squeeze,
This cheerful fruit aims to please.

In a sour moment, it turns the tide,
A zesty burst we cannot hide.
Laughter echoes, spreads far and wide,
With every slice, joy's our guide.

Joyful Squeezes

A wink from a fruit, oh so round,
Its citrusy wit knows no bound.
Bottled giggles, squeezed with glee,
Each zesty drop celebrates spree.

In the afternoon sun, it dances bright,
A little tease, quite the sight.
Puns like pulp, sweeter than pie,
As we chuckle, time slips by.

With a twist and a press, it starts to sing,
Spinning tales of the joy it can bring.
Sour moments melt in the sun,
With every squeeze, we have our fun.

Warmth Wrapped in Zest

Wrapped in warmth, a twist of fun,
This little fruit has just begun.
With zest so bright, and grin so wide,
It brings a spark we can't abide.

Tropical jokes, oh such a tease,
Witty slices, just what we need.
A jig in a jar, it spins around,
With a laugh that echoes, joy is found.

Refreshing tales in every bite,
Citrusy giggles, a pure delight.
Dance in the bowl, it's time to play,
This fruity friend brightens the day.

Citrus Auras

In sunny hues, a chuckle glows,
With every cut, the laughter flows.
Breezy breezes and sweet delight,
This lively orb sparks pure light.

Citrus capers in the air,
Fruity whispers, a funny flair.
On the table, it's quite the scene,
Lemon laughs, that's the routine.

Banishing gloom with zesty fun,
When life gets dull, it's number one.
Bursting with joy, so full of cheer,
This lively fruit is always near.

Warmth in Bitter

In a garden, citrus shy,
A yellow face caught my eye.
With a frown that turned to glee,
A tangy wink just for me.

Beneath the sun's bright embrace,
It laughed with a sun-kissed grace.
Sour tales spun with delight,
Joking with bees in flight.

A pucker followed by a grin,
Sassy leaves dance in the wind.
Life's zesty charms, no pretense,
It's a chuckle in its essence.

Sweetness hides amid the sour,
In the citrus kingdom's power.
Every twist, a laughter flute,
Joy found in the juicy fruit.

Twinkling Citrus Lights

In a bowl, they brightly shine,
A citrus spark, oh so divine.
Each a jest in vibrant hue,
A merry dance, in morning dew.

With rind that sings a playful tune,
Beneath the sun, they burst in June.
A ball of laughter round and bold,
Whispers sweet, yet tales unfold.

When life gives you twists and care,
Just squeeze a smile, show you dare.
Rolling joy in every bite,
They twinkle softly, pure delight.

At gatherings, they take the stage,
Witty fruits, set hearts ablaze.
Beneath the peel, a story grows,
Life delight, in citrus prose.

Whimsical Zest

In kitchens bright, they play their part,
A zesty wink, a citrus art.
With every chop, a giggle loud,
The juiciest fruit, it draws a crowd.

A sprinkle here, a dash of cheer,
Adds magic notes, they gleam sincere.
With laughter, they fill the air,
Whipped up fun, without a care.

Sour yet sweet, a comic twist,
A citrus punch you can't resist.
Like jester's hats on sunny days,
These bright guys chase the gloom away.

So raise your glass and make a toast,
To zesty laughs we love the most.
In silly moments, grooves and charms,
They'll steal your heart with sunny arms.

Bright Horizons

In fields of gold, a merry dream,
Chasing rays like a sunlit beam.
Each tangy burst, a giggly cheer,
Whispers of joy, always near.

With crescent smiles in every slice,
Citrusy giggles, oh so nice.
Round and bright in the morning glow,
Why so serious? Just let it flow.

As dawn arrives with zest anew,
They greet the day with a sunny view.
Sunkissed faces, a playful jest,
Lively moments that never rest.

So take a breath, embrace the day,
With zesty fun to light the way.
In every bite, and every laugh,
Find bright horizons on the path.

Juicy Laughter

In the garden, citrus cheer,
With a grin that brings good cheer.
Wobbling, jiggling in the breeze,
Brighter than a sunlit tease.

Yellow skin and zest to share,
Jokes that bounce from here to there.
Tarts and sweets in a fine blend,
A giggle from the fruit to send.

Brighter Days Ahead

When life hands you tangy rays,
Pucker up and seize the days.
Bouncing laughter, oh so bright,
Filling hearts with pure delight.

Clouds may come, they may just pass,
Like a prank that's made to last.
A twist, a squirt, the joy unfolds,
With sunshine, every tale retold.

Between Bitter and Sweet

In the citrus circus, too much fun,
A playful fight under the sun.
Tart and tangy, a dance surprise,
Witty jabs and silly cries.

Juices dribbling, laughter flows,
Each giggle blooms, the humor grows.
So don't fret when life seems tough,
A zesty punch can be enough.

Golden Light at Dusk

As the sun dips, colors gleam,
Citrus friends start to dream.
Under skies of orange glow,
Chasing shadows to and fro.

Mischief sparkles in the air,
Each burst of joy, a cheerful flare.
Golden laughter, sweet surprise,
Life's a joke in disguise.

The Brightness of Zest

Bright and yellow, round and bold,
A jester's cap, a tale retold.
Sour and sweet, a citrus jest,
Dancing on tongues, it's always best.

In salads tossed, it takes a leap,
With cheeky winks, it makes you peep.
Zesty giggles in every slice,
Who knew tartness could be so nice?

With every swirl, it twirls with glee,
In fizzy sips, it's wild and free.
A twist of fun, a laugh in store,
A playful zing, you'll always want more!

So raise a glass, let's toast today,
To the zest that brightens our way.
In laughter's glow, we find our cheer,
For in each bite, joy's always near.

Mirthful Sunshine

Yellow giggles in the air,
A cheeky prank, oh what a dare!
With patchwork smiles it beams so wide,
In every dish, it takes great pride.

Bouncing in pies, so light on feet,
A party guest, it can't be beat.
Zippy zest, a jolly tease,
It tickles tongues with such great ease.

In lemonade's embrace, it swirls,
A carnival of fun unfurls.
With every sip, we burst with laughter,
A zany twist is just the after.

So when you see that sunny hue,
Remember joy is waiting for you.
In every wedge, life's tart delight,
A smile appears, oh what a sight!

Radiance in Every Bite

A sunny ball of tangy cheer,
It brightens up, it brings good cheer.
With citrus pranks, it sings a tune,
A cheeky laugh beneath the moon.

In pastries sweet, it loves to play,
A hint of fun in every way.
With every squirt, it starts to shine,
A zippy grin, oh how divine!

In puddings thick, it finds its home,
A jester's heart in every dome.
A splash of joy, a chuckle bright,
It transforms meals into pure delight.

So gather round for a vibrant treat,
Where laughter and flavor joyfully meet.
In every slice and every bite,
The zest of life, a pure delight!

Glee in the Grove

In trees so tall, a playful spree,
Nature laughs with glee for free.
The sun-kissed fruits, so bright and round,
In every grove, joy can be found.

With playful peels, they twist and spin,
A shindig starts, let's all jump in!
In citrus storms, we dance around,
As laughter echoes, joy knows no bound.

A splash of zest in sassy pies,
Bright citrus dreams that never die.
From morning drinks to night's delight,
Giggling flavors take us to new heights.

So join the fun, don't be behind,
In lemony tales, bliss you'll find.
A grove of smiles all intertwined,
Where laughter reigns, and zest is kind!

Tangy Whispers

In a bowl of fruit, so bright and round,
Lurks a zesty joke, waiting to be found.
With a twist and a squint, it starts to grin,
A pucker of joy, let the fun begin!

When life gives you fruit, just peel it right,
Each slice holds a giggle, a burst of light.
Squeeze out the chuckles, let laughter reign,
A citrusy pun, sweetened by the rain!

The kitchen's alive, with a frothy cheer,
As zestful banter brings everybody near.
Joking around, we bite, we share,
In this tangy delight, there's love in the air!

So next time you see that sunny hue,
Remember the giggles it brings to you.
Laugh along, let the joy expand,
For this citrus trickster, it's all unplanned!

Radiant Citrus Laughter

A sunny ball rolls into the fray,
Its laughter contagious, bright as day.
With each juicy joke, it zestfully beams,
In the fruit bowl's party, it's all about dreams!

Peel back your worries, let humor unfold,
This merry orb's tales are pure gold.
With giggles galore, it spins round and round,
In a tangle of laughter, sweet joy is found.

When life feels too sour, grab this delight,
For a splash of fun, it's just so right.
With a chuckle and grin, we all take a sip,
In a glass of good cheer, let's take a trip!

So squeeze out your troubles, pour in the glee,
Raise a toast to the fruit that sets us free.
Let the laughter flow, it's a vibrant call,
In the world of citrus, there's room for us all!

Gleaming Rind

Oh, shiny sphere, so full of zest,
In your playful glow, we are truly blessed.
With a wink and a twist, you burst with glee,
Leaving us all smiling, happy as can be!

Peeling back layers, surprises unfold,
Each vibrant slice is a story retold.
In the dance of the kitchen, you sway and sing,
Bright flavor and laughter, you always bring.

Let's roll you around, just like a game,
Chasing the joy that never feels lame.
Your punchy humor makes cooking a treat,
With each little giggle, life's zest feels complete!

So gather the crew, let the laughter shine,
In the world of the zesty, everything's fine.
From spritzes of joy to a funny renown,
This gleaming delight wears the best crown!

Brightness in a Peel

Bright and cheerful, with a little twirl,
You brighten the day, oh my tangy pearl!
With laughter like sunshine, you lighten the load,
Every slice a joyride down laughter's road!

In kitchens galore, you're the life of the show,
Dancing with happiness, stealing the glow.
When life feels a bit stale, you're the remedy sweet,
A chuckle, a smile, that just can't be beat!

Squeeze out the worries, let giggles ignite,
With every sharp quip, you soar to new height.
In a citrusy whirlwind, we find our delight,
A burst of good humor, oh what a sight!

So toss in the laughter, sprinkle it right,
With joyful concoctions that feel just so bright.
Raise your glass high to this playful appeal,
For life's little wonders come wrapped in a peel!

Juicy Echoes

In a pantry of yellow, bright and bold,
Zesty jokes waiting, ripe and untold.
With a twist and a giggle, they burst with glee,
Sour faces will turn, just wait and see!

A splash of bright laughter, zestful and spry,
Juicy quips tumble under the sky.
From citrusy corners, the chuckles unfold,
Each slice a surprise, a treasure to hold!

With every fresh squeeze, the giggles ensue,
Tangy like mischief, good moods will renew.
Bouncing off bottles, the mirth it confides,
In the world of the tangy, joy never hides!

In the sunlit shade, where the laughter flows,
Ask the clever lemon, how funny it grows.
With a wink and a smile, it sprinkles delight,
In the heart of the kitchen, humor takes flight!

Cheerful Citrus Chorus

A chorus of citrus, bright in their cheer,
With zest on their lips, they spread good vibes here.
Squeezed out of laughter, the notes drip and dance,
Every tart little tune gives joy a chance!

In bowls of fresh fruit, the melodies pair,
Songs of the sunlight, painted with flair.
Together they harmonize, sassy and sweet,
An orchestra riot that can't be beat!

In this playful banquet, all flavors unite,
Banishing gloom, making sour take flight.
From cheerful displays, their stories unfurl,
A citrusy jest, a spin of the world!

So raise up your glasses, let laughter collide,
In a splash of vivacity, no reason to hide.
Each sip brings a giggle; a joyful encore,
As the cheerful chorus leaves smiles galore!

Soft Sunlight and Sourness

Soft sunlight spills over, bringing the joy,
While sly little lemons just wait to employ.
Their bright little snickers, they shine with a wink,
Mixing sweet rays with a giggle or drink!

Sourness emerges from shadows to greet,
With playful charm, they jiggle and meet.
In gardens of laughter, their brightness is found,
Soft petals of humor drift lightly around!

A squirt of mischief from their joyful zest,
Turning lemons to laughter, they know how to jest.
In the dance of the afternoon, sunny and free,
Sour transforms into sweet, all giggles agree!

So gather the brightness, let spirits unwind,
Where sunlight and laughter leave sourness blind.
With the zest of the season, each moment convenes,
In the sparkling laughter, happiness gleans!

Slices of Happiness

On a plate of joy, slices sparkle and gleam,
Citrus smiles twinkle, inspiring the dream.
Each wedge a reminder of moments so bright,
Turning ordinary days into pure delight!

With each playful nibble, the laughter expands,
Flavorful joy slips through curious hands.
In every fresh cut, a giggle appears,
Slicing through troubles, dispelling our fears!

Tossed in a salad, or drank with a cheer,
Each tangy creation brings loved ones near.
From piquant to juicy, they dance on the tongue,
Chasing away blues, where laughter is sung!

So gather your friends, and let the feast flow,
With slices of sparkle, enjoy every glow.
For happiness thrives in the silliness found,
In those citrusy slices, joy knows no bounds!

Happiness Infused

In the orchard, colors gleam,
Laughter bursts like a dream.
Sour notes dance in the air,
Life's a joke—it's only fair.

Bursting pith with a twist,
Sunshine caught in a fist.
Grab a slice, take a bite,
Everything feels just right.

Juicy tales, a tangy tease,
Life's a circus, do as you please.
Bright yellow smiles everywhere,
Join the fun, if you dare!

In the glass, a citrus cheer,
Sipping joy with a sneer.
A splash of zest, oh so bold,
Makes the mundane turn to gold.

Sunshine Served Fresh.

A citrus crown upon my head,
Under the sun, we all are fed.
Silly faces that never tire,
Lemon antics, we conspire.

With every bite, a giggle grows,
Sour bursts, and laughter flows.
Jumping juices, what a sight,
Turn a frown into delight!

Squeeze the day with all your might,
Chase your troubles, take a flight.
Bright and zesty, oh so sweet,
A comedy in every treat!

Life's absurd, and that's the game,
Making clowns of all the same.
So raise your glass, start the fun,
Citrus smiles for everyone!

Citrus Grins

When life gives you vibrant hue,
Turn it bright, shake off the blue.
A cheeky zest, a playful bite,
Citrus glee is pure delight.

On a plate, they dance and play,
Gorilla smiles at end of day.
Peel away the mundane vibe,
Sour chuckles start to jibe.

Hands sticky with the juice of cheer,
Sliced in wedges, laughter near.
A funny tale, a slice of fun,
Join the party, everyone!

Citrus magic, quite absurd,
Spreading joy, not a word.
Let's all giggle, giggle loud,
Snap a pic, let's be proud!

Zesty Whispers

In a world that's sweet and sour,
Zesty whispers bloom like a flower.
Citrus giggles light the way,
Turning dull to bright each day.

Rolling lemons on the ground,
Bouncing high with joyful sound.
A punchline here, a burst of zest,
Silly moments are the best.

Juicy pranks behind the stand,
Sour surprises, oh so grand.
With a twist, we share a laugh,
Celebrations, on our behalf.

Every wedge a slice of fun,
Zesty chills, and then we run.
Sunshine's glow upon our face,
Join the fray, this citrus chase!

Refreshing Solstice

Bright citrus hangs, so bold and round,
A zesty jester, joy is found,
With every squeeze, a laugh will burst,
In sunny days, we quench our thirst.

Lemonade stands on every street,
Sipping sweet, can't be beat,
A twist of fate in every glass,
We raise our cups and toast with sass.

Citrus cheer in every bite,
A radiant snack, oh what a sight,
With puckerings that make us grin,
A whimsy world where fun begins.

So let's parade in yellow hues,
With juicy whispers, we can't lose,
As laughter dances in the air,
The sun shines bright, without a care.

Smiles from Nature's Bounty

In orchards lush, they gleefully swing,
Golden globes with a delightful zing,
Nature's jesters, in sunlit rows,
Every bite, pure laughter flows.

Zesty drops fall like joyful rain,
A burst of fun that drives us sane,
In every dish, they take the stage,
Shining smiles, we turn the page.

Cakes and pies with a tarty twist,
Each taste explosion is too hard to resist,
A slice of joy, like laughter's call,
With every meal, they thrill us all.

We gather 'round for citrus cheer,
With joyful hearts, we hold them dear,
Nature's bounty, a funny treat,
In our smiles, they can't be beat.

Radiant Fruit

Tiny suns hide in leafy green,
Their vibrant glow is quite the scene,
Round and cheerful, a giggling gem,
Nature's joy, our favorite friend.

Sliced in halves, they create delight,
A tangy burst in each daylight,
Sprinkled with sugar, a laughter fest,
Oh, how they humor, they are the best!

Picnics thrive with zesty fun,
Playing games till day is done,
Every squeeze a playful jest,
With radiant fruit, we are blessed.

So dance and twirl, let's celebrate,
The cheerful hues that we create,
In every dish, a pucker here,
Our hearts are light, our minds are clear.

Tangy Reflections

In the garden, a curious sight,
Sunny orbs that shine so bright,
Their peels conceal such lively humor,
With tangy tastes, their laugh we tour.

Sipping nectar, we can't refrain,
Each juicy drop, a funny gain,
They wink and pucker, oh what a tease,
Brightening moments, a zestful breeze.

With sparkling drinks and jiggly cakes,
They bring the fun, no room for fakes,
As laughter echoes through the air,
With every treat, we've not a care.

So gather round, and share a laugh,
With citrus joys, we find our path,
In nature's wit, we live and thrive,
In tangy moments, we feel alive.

A Touch of Brightness

In a fruit bowl, there sits a clown,
With a yellow grin, he won't frown.
He chuckles at apples, ripe and round,
Squeezed out joy in every sound.

A twist of zest in every game,
Bright citrus laughter keeps the same.
With every slice, a smile to share,
Who knew a fruit could truly care?

Juicy jests in every drop,
Rolling laughter, non-stop.
In sunshine's glow, he takes a stand,
The happiest fruit in all the land!

So when you're down, and life's a grind,
Look to the bowl, and you will find,
A burst of sunshine, a giggle spree,
In the jester's face, so wild and free.

Sweetness in Drought

When the sky is gray and hopes turn thin,
A yellow wonder, let the fun begin!
A tangy twist, a laughter spree,
With every sip, life's lemon tea.

In the pantry, a treasure lies,
With a silly grin that never dies.
A splash of zest, oh what a treat,
Turning dry days into something sweet.

Amidst the gloom, he dances bright,
Turning the frown into delight.
Squeeze out trouble, mix in some cheer,
With every laugh, the drought disappears.

So take a taste, embrace the fun,
A sunny heart in everyone.
Beneath his skin, laughter's found,
Sweetness in drought, joy all around.

Serenade of Juicy Bliss

In the kitchen, a symphony plays,
A serenade of lemony days.
With a twist and a squeeze, oh what a show,
This fruity solo steals the glow!

Bouncing around, he's got the beat,
Squelching worries, life's bittersweet.
Let's dance to the rhythm, bright and clear,
With juicy laughter, we have no fear.

When life gives you woes, take a sip,
Let the juice be your merry trip.
He'll tickle your tongue, make you grin wide,
In juicy bliss, there's nothing to hide!

So raise a glass, let's toast this friend,
With lemon laughter, joy has no end.
In the notes of citrus, we find our glee,
A serenade of bliss, wild and free.

Citrusy Sighs

Oh, citrus dreams on a sunny day,
With a chuckle or two, we'll find our way.
A wink from the peel, a giggle galore,
In the zest of life, we always want more.

With a squirt of fun in every bite,
Life's sour notes become a delight.
A twisty dance, so bright and spry,
These citrusy sighs will make you fly!

Through snickers and grins, we hoot and cheer,
Even the bitter can bring out a tear.
So in the kitchen, let joy ignite,
With a lemon's charm, we'll soar like a kite!

As we share this joy, let laughter ring,
In every citrus heart, what bliss we bring.
So join the fun, don't let it shy,
With citrusy sighs, we'll always try!

Sun-Kissed Radiance

In the garden, a bright little sphere,
Sunshine dances, spreading good cheer.
With a grin like a jester so spry,
Tickling taste buds as it zips by.

Juggling flavors with zest and flair,
Bouncing around without a care.
It rolls and tumbles, a playful tease,
Squeezing giggles with each little breeze.

Bright yellow laughter fills the air,
Turning frowns into joyous stares.
A twist of mischief, a burst of glee,
Oh, what a sight for all to see!

Amidst the fruits, it reigns supreme,
Crafting smiles like a sunny dream.
Oh radiant wonder, so full of fun,
A slice of happiness under the sun!

Tangy Joy

A zesty bubble wrapped in peel,
Spritzing sunshine with every meal.
It winks at you from the fruit bowl high,
A tangy jester, oh my, oh my!

With a hop and a roll, it leads the way,
Bringing giggles to each sunny day.
Gentle bursts of laughter, so bright,
Its comedic charm is pure delight.

Sour meets sweet in a playful dance,
Inviting everyone to take a chance.
It spritzes humor on each plate,
A cheeky smile that simply can't wait!

In recipes grand, or as simple treat,
This ball of joy is quite the feat.
With every slice, it's clear to see,
Life's better when you're zestily free!

Bright Drops of Cheer

A splash of sunshine in the sky,
Cascading laughter as it stands by.
It lights up dreams with a cheeky grin,
Leaving traces of joy, where to begin?

Rolling around with glee in its core,
A jolly prankster we all adore.
One drop of nectar, and giggles ensue,
A bubbling giggle, fresh and anew.

In lemonade glasses or baked treats bright,
It tickles the tongue with pure delight.
Through ups and downs, it's always near,
This sunny orb filled with sheer cheer!

So raise a toast to this glowing sphere,
Adding sweetness to every year.
With every bite, it's plain to see,
Bright drops of joy forever will be!

Golden Citrus Gleam

In a grove where funny faces grow,
A golden gem puts on a show.
With antics bold, it leaps and spins,
Bursting the monotony, fun begins!

It paints the world in lemony hue,
Witty and clever, like a chuckle, too.
Every squeeze brings a pop of delight,
As laughter echoes from morning to night.

Wobbling and wobbling, it makes its way,
Tickling taste buds in the silliest way.
With every slice, hilarity blooms,
Filling our kitchens with joyful tunes.

So here's to the fruits of golden cheer,
Whispering secrets for all to hear.
With zest and spirit, it lives in esteem,
This citrus treasure, a giggly dream!

Sunshine's Slice

A twisty grin that can't be beat,
A sunny shine that's quite a treat.
With zesty jokes and citrus cheer,
It brightens up the atmosphere.

In every drop, a giggle's found,
Where laughter leaves its tangy sound.
Sour friends with sunny glee,
Bring smiles as sweet as can be!

A slice of joy on every plate,
Life's lemony little fate.
With every squirt, a burst of fun,
Let's soak in rays till day is done!

So grab a glass and take a sip,
Let's laugh and dance, we'll take a trip.
In citrus worlds, where gags abide,
A zesty journey, come for the ride!

Brightness Served Chilled

Frosty mugs with citrus zest,
Quenching thirst, it's simply the best.
A giggle here, a chuckle there,
Brighten up with frothy flair.

Lemon drops in playful spins,
Sip and laugh, let joy begin.
Each bubble pops with silly dreams,
A carnival of citrus beams.

Chilled to perfection, the laughter flows,
With punchlines that give rosy nose.
So raise a glass, here's to the fun,
With every sip, you'll feel like won!

Join the dance of zestful glee,
In a world where we're wild and free.
Each laugh a slice of happiness,
In a chilled cup of bright excess!

Delicate Dew on Citrus

Morning glimmers, dew so light,
On citrus smiles, a pure delight.
A playful wink from nature's crown,
As day unfolds its sunny gown.

Laughter dances on the breeze,
With citrus flowers buzzing bees.
Dewdrops twinkle like silly stars,
In the garden where giggles are.

As playful squirrels join the fun,
They bounce and leap, on the run.
Each zesty burst a joyful sound,
In nature's stage, where laughs abound!

So when you see that dew's embrace,
Think of joy in every place.
With a citrus grin, let's not be shy,
Let's spread the laughter, oh my, oh my!

Mirth Beneath Citrus Skies

Under arches of citrus bliss,
Giggles swirl in a sunny kiss.
Each cloud a balloon, floating high,
With little laughs that never die.

The sky is splashed with vibrant cheer,
A citrus party, it's crystal clear.
Jokes dangle like fruit on a vine,
Let's savor laughter, oh how divine!

Beneath the branches, we sit and play,
With tangerine tales that brighten the day.
In the shade, we sip with ease,
Savoring every moment that teases!

So grab a friend, come join the spree,
Under citrus skies, we're wild and free.
Let's chuckle away the hours so bright,
With joyful hearts, we'll dance in light!

Sweet and Sour Delight

In a bowl of sunshine bright,
Looking oh so cheerfully tight,
A zesty grin with a twist,
How could you resist this list?

With a splash that brings a laugh,
Sour faced yet full of gaff,
Rolling on the kitchen floor,
Who knew fruit could start a war?

A chuckle from the bitter bite,
Dancing through the day and night,
Sipping on a tangy drink,
Who knew laughter was the link?

A citrus joke in every slice,
Juicy puns are always nice,
When life gives you jokes so fine,
You simply add a twist of rhyme.

Laughter in the Orchard

In the grove where laughter grows,
A ticklish breeze, the fun it shows,
Branches swaying, fruits collide,
The merry hum of joy and pride.

Citrus giggles in the air,
A yellow jester without a care,
Jokes on wind, like seeds they're cast,
Making memories that will last.

Each fruit a comedian in its own right,
With punchlines waiting for the night,
When the stars in laughter gleam,
And all of nature starts to beam.

Come join us in this fruity dance,
With silly winks and a glance,
For in this orchard, joy you'll find,
A fruity giggle shared, so kind.

Vibrant Citrus Dance

Wobbling on the kitchen shelf,
An orange ball with a zesty self,
Spinning round, it jives and prances,
In a fragrant citrus dance of chances.

Witty pips and juicy cheer,
Bouncing whimsies everywhere,
Lemonade dreams and zestful glee,
Who knew fruit could be so free?

A vibrant blend of laughter bright,
Squeezed in sunlight, sheer delight,
Sugary grins make spirits lift,
A delightful, tangy gift.

So join this merry, funny spree,
With fruity friends so wild and free,
In every twist, a giggle blooms,
As laughter dances in the rooms.

Glow of Freshness

A glimmer shines upon the peel,
With merry zest that makes us squeal,
Ticklish tangs in every bite,
A fruity glow that feels just right.

Lemon lights with giggles bright,
In the fridge, a tasty sight,
Juicy freshness on the tongue,
In the kitchen, songs are sung.

Sour notes make rush and flip,
With laughter flowing in each sip,
A potion brewed from pure delight,
That tingles through the day and night.

So when you seek a fruity grin,
Look for the sunshine tucked within,
For in each slice, you'll find the key,
To savor life and set it free.

Sunlight on the Tongue

A slice of yellow, bright and bold,
Dancing around like stories told.
Zesty giggles in a sunny spree,
Winking at me from the citrus tree.

Sipping sunshine in a cup,
Making frowns turn quickly up.
Puckered cheeks and laughter flow,
Oh, what a show, what a glow!

Rolling laughter, round and sweet,
A citrus tango on my feet.
Each squirt a laugh, each taste a cheer,
Spreading joy from ear to ear.

When life gives you tangy gifts,
Twist and twirl, give joy some lifts.
With every wedge, a new delight,
Bringing chuckles, pure and bright.

Juiced Joys

Squeeze the day, let laughter out,
Pulp of joy, that's what it's about!
Glasses raised in a fruity cheer,
Every sip brings giggles near.

Zingy splashes in the air,
Playful jests without a care.
Piquant notes dance in a line,
Making breakfast taste divine.

Sour surprises on the tongue,
Tickling senses; oh, so fun!
Every drop a chuckle bright,
Serving smiles with morning light.

A carnival of flavors twist,
In every jug, a giggling mist.
Juicy joys spill all around,
Life's a laugh — so sweet, unbound!

Citrus Infusion

In every pinch, a jest unfolds,
Golden secrets the citrus holds.
Spritzed with mirth, a fizzy spree,
Sharing giggles, just you and me.

Wedges clink like glasses raised,
To the laughter we have praised.
Bubbling joy, a citrus drink,
Swirling smiles in every blink.

With every zesty twist, we find,
Life's quirky jokes, one of a kind.
Punny flavors, tangy delight,
Turning frowns to sheer delight.

Mix and mingle, squirt and splash,
Citrus chaos in a dash.
Round and round, our spirits soar,
Unleashing giggles — who could ask for more?

Glistening Yellows

A shimmer bright upon the plate,
Chasing dullness, it can't wait.
Zingy splashes, cheerful sights,
Witty bursts, oh what delights!

Yellow laughter fills the room,
Filling hearts, dispelling gloom.
With every bite, the fun extends,
Crisp and curvy, the joy transcends.

Sunny smiles in bubbly form,
Drenched in giggles, a quirky norm.
Every splash is pure delight,
Citrus magic shining bright.

From peels to pips, the joy is real,
Tasting laughter with every meal.
Bright and bold, a memory made,
In every corner, fun displayed.

Sweet and Sour Serenade

In a bowl of joy, it dips and spins,
Its zestful grin makes laughter win.
Sour notes dance, the taste buds cheer,
A citrus clown, we all hold dear.

With a twist and a squirt, it takes the stage,
In lemony antics, it's all the rage.
Bright yellow face, pure mischief style,
Bringing giggles, oh what a smile!

Dressed in sunshine, it skips around,
In kitchens worldwide, it's truly renowned.
Pies and drinks, it's the star of the show,
Wherever it goes, good vibes in tow!

A little tartness, a touch of cheer,
It spritzes fun, parades the year.
Join in the laughter, don't be shy,
With each zesty burst, let your spirits fly!

Sunshine in a Peel

A cheerful glow in the fruit bowl lies,
With a wink and a squeeze, it teases the eyes.
Bouncing on tables, it rolls with glee,
A happiness orb for all to see.

In pitchers it swirls, a bubbly affair,
Around summer nights, it fills the air.
Happy hour calls, with sips filled with cheer,
Its citrusy giggles bring friends near.

Bright as a sunbeam, with zestful flair,
It juggles good moments without a care.
When life gets sour, it's quick to remind,
A twist in our fate, the sweet we can find.

Oh peels of gold, keep the laughter alive,
With your sunny spirit, we all will thrive.
In every squeeze, a story unfurls,
Creating bright smiles that swirl and twirl!

A Burst of Brightness

A pop of zest, a jolt of cheer,
It brings forth giggles from far and near.
With a squirt of joy, it twirls and plays,
A cheeky prankster in citrus arrays.

In salads, in drinks, it reigns supreme,
A vibrant friend, living the dream.
With each little burst, it tickles the tongue,
In every good pun, its laughter is sung.

It winks from the bowl, a mischief-filled sight,
Turning dull moments to pure delight.
With a smile so bright, it's hard to resist,
A tangy reminder of joy we should list.

In the circus of flavors, it plays a key role,
A slapstick delight for every soul.
So let's raise a glass, cheers to its finesse,
In every squeeze, we find happiness!

Lemonade Dreams

In dreams of sweetness, a splash appears,
A bright yellow vision that tickles our cheers.
A tart little dream in a glass so cold,
Refreshing adventures waiting to unfold.

With ice cubes dancing, it shimmies with zest,
A bubbly companion, it's simply the best.
Each sip a giggle, each gulp pure delight,
In this carnival of flavors, everything's bright.

Imagine a world where lemons take flight,
Zooming and zipping, pure joy in sight.
They prank the sad clouds, chase tears away,
Creating a rainbow at the end of the day.

So pour a tall glass, let the fun begin,
Raise your cups high, let the party spin!
With laughter and zest, let the moments gleam,
In the land of lemons, we'll always dream.

A Dance of Flavor

A yellow orb spins on the plate,
With a wink that's truly first-rate.
Faces scrunch in zestful cheer,
As laughter erupts from far and near.

It jiggles in a fruity ballet,
Swaying to tunes of the sunny bay.
A curious child takes a bite,
Flavors twirling in pure delight.

With every squirt, giggles ignite,
A pucker, a dance, of sheer delight.
A citrus party, bright and bold,
A zesty tale to be retold.

A sunny grin from a playful slice,
Mocking your face, oh isn't it nice?
Join the feast or miss the cheer,
This yellow jest draws all near.

Serendipitous Citrus

A twisty fruit with a playful guise,
Hides secrets in its sunny sighs.
Discovering joy in each tangy drop,
A giggle here, a chortle nonstop.

With every slice, it sparks some fun,
A zesty joke from its golden run.
It tickles tongues with tasty rays,
Bringing laughter to ordinary days.

Oh, the moments when joy's unleashed,
As tangy bites make worries ceased.
A slice of whimsy, bright and spry,
Life is sweeter; oh, my, oh my!

When life gives you this yellow treat,
Don't take it serious, just feel the beat.
Dance with the fruit, let humor abide,
In this playful citrus ride.

Whirlwind of Zest

In a colorful bowl, they convene,
Jovial orbs, the zestful scene.
With a swirl of laughter, they greet,
And set the mood with a citrus beat.

It's a party of flavors, emotions collide,
As slices bounce and twirl with pride.
A tutorial of joy, lessons in sass,
Even the dullest moments they surpass.

With a splash, they explode into glee,
A taste of fun, wild and free.
Jokes on your palate, oh what a twist,
In this whirlwind, you can't resist.

So take a seat and share the fun,
With a splash of zest for everyone.
Lively laughter, let's all agree,
Life's sweeter when shared with glee.

Radiant Joys of Nature

A sun-kissed fruit with a vibrant grin,
Whispering tales of the joys within.
Brought to life in a playful dance,
A zesty chance for a merry prance.

In the gardens where colors bloom,
This bright delight can lift the gloom.
It's not just food; it's pure delight,
A radiant spark on a sunny sight.

From morning sips to evening treats,
Each burst of flavor cracks the seats.
With every chuckle, every cheer,
Nature's jest brings you near.

So savor the zest, embrace the fun,
Join in the laughter, let's all run.
With every glow that nature styles,
Our hearts become bright, full of smiles.

Cheerful Drops

In the garden, round and bright,
A citrus orb, a pure delight.
It winks at bees with zestful cheer,
A fruity prankster, oh so dear.

With every squeeze, a giggle spills,
On summer days, it plays with thrills.
A splash of joy in every sip,
This jolly fruit demands a trip.

Sunshine on the Tongue

A burst of sunshine in each bite,
With giggles dancing, oh what a sight!
Sour notes that tickle the mind,
A zesty laugh, so well-defined.

It rolls and bounces, full of glee,
Creating smiles, just you and me.
With every twist, a playful jest,
This citrus cheer is truly the best.

Golden Glow of Happiness

Radiant yellow, bright as the sun,
A citrus treasure, oh what fun!
It laughs in bowls, a jolly show,
In every kitchen, that golden glow.

Sprinkled on treats, a zippy zing,
It brings the joy that sweetens everything.
A jibe and jolt, it lifts the mood,
This happy fruit, we're all imbued.

Juicy Revelations

Secrets whispered from within,
When squeezed just right, they make us grin.
Pulp surprises, juicy and bright,
A comedy act, a sheer delight.

In every glass, a giggly cheer,
Each tiny drop spreads joy so near.
With zesty tales on every tongue,
This fruit knows how to have some fun.

Citrus Grin

A cheeky fruit upon the shelf,
Its vibrant hue, a glowing elf.
With pucker and a zesty cheer,
It brings forth giggles, far and near.

Sipping juice, it makes us laugh,
A tangy twist, a citrus craft.
In lemonade, it finds its voice,
And every sip, we make a choice.

Its peels are bright, a sunny dance,
A smile that puts us in a trance.
With every bite, our spirits rise,
A joke wrapped up in sunny guise.

So here's to you, bright citrus friend,
In laughter, you will never end.
With silly faces, we all play,
A zestful heart that's here to stay.

Zestful Laughter

A tangy joke upon my plate,
With every slice, it's sure to rate.
The citrus giggles in the sun,
Each bite a bop, oh what a fun!

With every squeeze, it drops a pun,
A fruity jest that's second to none.
From gardens bright with golden flair,
It tickles noses, fills the air.

In summer light, it plays its part,
That sunny grin warms every heart.
When life is sour, just take a taste,
In every laugh, there's no time to waste.

So raise a glass and toast in cheer,
To laughter shared, and friends drawn near.
A citrus burst, we sing and sway,
In joyful zest, we play all day.

Sunlit Slices

Bright wedges on my kitchen board,
A sunny cheer, can't be ignored.
It winks and shines, a playful tease,
With curvy smiles, it aims to please.

Squirting juice like nature's fun,
With every drop, it's laughter spun.
In summer's light, it feels so right,
A toast to friendship, pure delight!

The zesty tang is quite a treat,
In playful banter, can't be beat.
As we slice through, the giggles grow,
With sunlit joy, our spirits flow.

So here we stand, a fruity crew,
With smiles so wide, we both just knew.
In every slice, a tale is spun,
Life's sweetest moments have just begun.

Joy in Yellow

In gardens lush, a yellow glow,
A happy fruit that steals the show.
With radiant zest, it laughs at gloom,
And fills our hearts, a sunny bloom.

Its quirky face, a joyful spark,
A burst of fun that leaves its mark.
We squeeze it tight, our spirits rise,
In every chuckle, sweet surprise.

From morning juice to afternoon,
It shares its light, a bright balloon.
When life gets tough, just take a slice,
In giggles shared, it makes things nice.

So lift a glass, let laughter flow,
In every sip, our joy will grow.
With yellow cheer, we'll dance and sing,
To the lively tune that good vibes bring.

Nature's Lively Harvest

In the orchard, laughter sings,
Bouncing fruits on vibrant swings.
Juicy jokes upon the trees,
Tickled leaves in playful breeze.

Each round fruit a wink, a jest,
Nature's party, simply the best!
With every peel a giggle hides,
As sunshine dances, joy abides.

Golden globes in bright array,
Juggling sweetness in the day.
Life's a joke, come take a bite,
Taste the laughter, pure delight!

Fun in every burst and squirt,
Nature grins beneath the dirt.
In every groan of zest in flight,
Harvests cheerfully ignite!

Fragrant Sunlight

Softly glowing, bright and bold,
Citrus charm, a tale retold.
Witty bursts that tickle noses,
Fragrant giggles that everyone knows us.

In sunlit patches, humor sprawls,
Glistening laughter as the vine calls.
A zesty play upon the tongue,
Songs of sweetness forever sung.

Mirth and blossoms intertwine,
Dancing rays of golden shine.
A citrus blush on eager cheeks,
Nature's laughter, joy she speaks.

Beneath bright skies, a joke unwinds,
In every slice, a grin you'll find.
Warmth of sun, a bright surprise,
Wrapped in giggles, happiness flies!

Tantalizing Tales of Sunshine

In golden fields, the sunlight beams,
Whispers of laughter float in dreams.
Fruitful tales in shadows play,
Joking branches sway and sway.

Chortles ripen with each vine,
Spin the stories, sweet and fine.
Zesty puns in citrus hues,
Nature's fun, your heart it woos.

Round and ripe, they slip and slide,
Juicy secrets they can't hide.
Every bite's a smile displayed,
In every twist, the fun portrayed.

Bursting stories, laughter's call,
Each embrace, a joyful thrall.
A banquet rich with sunshine's style,
A feast of joy, a citrus smile!

Citrus Celebration

Gather round for a juicy cheer,
Life's a festival, spread the sphere!
Fruity giggles in every glass,
Joyous feasts that come to pass.

Zingy flavors, pure delight,
Celebrate from day to night.
With each squeeze, a grin appears,
Raise a toast and toast your peers!

A splash of fun, a zesty prank,
Citrus jokes in drink and tank.
Sunkissed smiles that fill the air,
Joyful moments everywhere!

Fruits of cheer in waves abound,
Dance and laughter all around.
Citrus champions in parade,
Join the fun, let fortune cascade!

Citrus Joyride

In a world of zest and fun,
Where oranges race and lemons run,
They jig and jive in sunlit glee,
A citrus party—come join me!

With juicy jokes and sour pranks,
They gather 'round in laughter's ranks,
Peeling back their joyful skins,
In this parade, everyone wins!

The limes do cartwheels, bold and bright,
While grapefruits dance to pure delight,
A splash of laughter fills the air,
In their fruity world, they have no care!

As day turns sweet with citrus cheer,
They raise a toast that all can hear,
With every sip, a wink of sun,
In this joyride, we're all young!

Lemony Daydreams

In dreams so bright, a yellow hue,
Silly thoughts like bubbles flew,
Giggling fruit in playful schemes,
They bounce along in lemon beams.

With zestful laughs and citrus tone,
In fields of yellow, joy is grown,
Each twist and turn, a chuckle shared,
In this world, no one is scared.

They swirl and twirl, with playful flair,
A lemon dance in fragrant air,
The sun's a giggle, warm and free,
Embracing all in harmony.

In every corner, laughter rings,
As nature's jester spreads its wings,
In daydreams bold and brightly spun,
Life's lemon laugh has just begun!

Sunkissed Smiles

A golden sun with laughter bright,
Brings out the smiles, a sheer delight,
With every rays, a giggle flows,
In fields of sunshine, joy just grows.

The fruit parade in radiant style,
Wearing smiles that stretch a mile,
They jostle, bounce, and shake around,
In their bright world, fun is found.

With a wink from oranges up high,
And funny faces, oh me, oh my!
They squeeze the day with wit and cheer,
In cheeky games from far and near.

Sunkissed antics take their flight,
Under the skies, all feels just right,
With two left feet, and one big scream,
These silly fruits fulfill the dream!

Cheerful Orchard Tales

In an orchard filled with beaming fruit,
Each tale is sweet, oh, what a hoot!
Laughter dances in the breeze,
With every joke, it's sure to please.

Grapes joke about their tiny size,
While peaches roll with giggling cries,
The lemons play a prank or two,
In this orchard, fun is true!

With apples crafting silly rhymes,
Time races by in joyful chimes,
A harvest full of laughter waits,
In their fruity space, joy creates.

Underneath the leafy shade,
Every smile and chuckle made,
In cheerful tales, together we sing,
In this lively orchard, joy takes wing!

Whimsy in a Spritz

In the garden, bright and zesty,
A jester's laugh, oh how it's messy.
With every squirt, a giggle grows,
Sunshine dances where the citrus flows.

Mischievous trees in a playful show,
Winking at bees that buzz to and fro.
Lemonade rivers in silly streams,
Tickling toes and igniting dreams.

A splash of joy, a twist of fate,
Where tangy antics create a plate.
Citrus capers in every cup,
Raise your glass, let's drink it up!

So gather round for a jolly fest,
In a world where sour is truly blessed.
With laughs and zings, we'll cheer and sway,
In this zany realm, let's play all day.

Tart Joys

Beneath the sun, a yellow grin,
Crafting mischief from within.
With cheeks so round and peels so bright,
They burst with jokes, pure delight.

Sour faces, sweetened replies,
Chasing giggles beneath the skies.
Each twist and turn, a twist of fate,
These funky fruits never hesitate.

Laughter spills like juice from a cup,
In every squeeze, we lift it up.
Dancing rays of citrus glow,
Spreading humor in a playful flow.

So here's a toast, let's drink to cheer,
To all the fun we hold so dear.
With every frolic, pure delight,
Tart joys flicker; Oh, what a sight!

Nature's Cheerful Fruit

Among the leaves, they catch the sun,
With chuckles rising, oh what fun!
Draped in sunshine, they plot and scheme,
Crafting giggles in a vibrant dream.

Their zest awakens sleepy days,
While dancing ants join in the plays.
Sour makes sweet in a comic twist,
Nature's jesters, they can't be missed.

With every wedge, surprise ignites,
Shining like stars on cozy nights.
Puns as juicy as their core,
Nature's laughter we can't ignore.

A toast to fun, we raise our glass,
As sunny spirits let good times pass.
Oh, nature's wonders, bright and free,
With every smile, it's pure glee!

Citrus Serenade

In the orchard, where laughter blooms,
Zany tunes chase away glooms.
Peeling layers of zest and cheer,
With citrus giggles drawing near.

Dancing fruits in a band of glee,
Singing tunes of jubilee.
Slipping notes of sour and sweet,
A medley that can't be beat.

With every slice, a zesty tune,
Bouncing lightly like a balloon.
Squeezed out laughter from rind so bright,
Twinkling joy in every bite.

Join the chorus, raise your voice,
In this citrus world, we rejoice.
For every laugh and every smile,
Let's sing along in funky style!

Lively Bounty of the Grove

In the grove where lemons dance,
A citrus party, all in pants.
They giggle bright upon the trees,
Dressed in yellow, swaying with ease.

The bees join in with buzzing cheer,
As lemons laugh, they have no fear.
With every twist, a wink they throw,
A zestful show, a vibrant glow.

Pick one up, give it a squeeze,
Watch the laughter in the breeze.
Their playful pucker spreads the sun,
In this grove, there's just pure fun!

So join the frolic, don't be shy,
Underneath the brightened sky.
In this lively, zesty place,
Find joy in lemon's quirky grace!

Golden Drops of Happiness

A sunny day, the fruits are bold,
Golden drops, a story told.
In every grin, a spark of cheer,
As zest and laughter fill the air.

With every sip, a twist of fate,
Sour and sweet can really bate.
Their juice is like a jolly song,
Refreshing taste that sings along.

Throw a party, let it go,
Dancing lemons, putting on a show.
In this world, a fun parade,
With golden drops, let's not be swayed!

So raise your glass, let laughter bubble,
In lemon land, there's no trouble.
A toast to joy, to every smile,
With these golden drops, let's stay awhile!

Tangy Tapestries

Behold the tapestry so bright,
Of lemons weaving pure delight.
With every twist, a giggle grows,
In humor's play, the tanginess glows.

Stitching joy in each yellow seam,
Their zesty charm, a lively dream.
Tangled threads of laughter swirl,
As lemons dance and hearts unfurl.

In a patchwork of citrus fun,
Every day feels like a pun.
A tapestry of sweet and sour,
Lemons shine with every hour.

So grab a slice, and let's create,
Together friendship, never late.
With tangy tales upon the shelf,
We laugh and cheer, we love ourselves!

Citrus Crescendos

In the orchards where they play,
Citrus crescendos brighten day.
With laughter bouncing off the leaves,
The world feels light, as joy retrieves.

Each little fruit, a joyful plea,
To dance with zest, be wild and free.
With every splash, a burst of cheer,
Sweet sunshine vibes are always near.

An orchestra of zing and zest,
With citrus notes, we feel the best.
A harmony of smiles and fun,
In every drop, we are all one!

So let the citrus serenade,
Fill our hearts, let worries fade.
For in this grove, we soar so high,
With citrus crescendos, laughter flies!

www.ingramcontent.com/pod-product-compliance
Lightning Source LLC
Chambersburg PA
CBHW060112230426
43661CB00003B/158